C000215255

The
Und
of
Exeter

Todd Gray

THE MINT PRESS

First published in Great Britain by The Mint Press, 2001

© Todd Gray & The Mint Press 2001

The right of Todd Gray to be identified as author of this work has been asserted by him in accordance with the Copyright, Designs & Patents Act 1988.

ISBN 1–903356–14–8

Cataloguing in Publication Data
CIP record for this title is available from the British Library

The Mint Press
18 The Mint
Exeter, Devon
England EX4 3BL

Text and cover design by Delphine Jones

Main cover illustration, Exeter match sellers by George Townsend, late nineteenth century courtesy of Westcountry Studies Library (MD, PD43605)

Printed and bound in Great Britain
by Short Run Press Ltd, Exeter.

CONTENTS

The Victorian Under Class *of* Exeter

FOREWORD

Exeter's poor, described in this book, typifies
such areas the length and breadth of the British
Isles and it was all happening when Britain was
Great, principally during the reign of Queen
Victoria (1837 –1901). One reads that it was
good to be around during the life and times of
Victoria. We had an empire which circled the
world. People lived in grand houses and led
lives to match. The industrial revolution was
upon us and everyone was doing well! But,
cheek to jowl with the affluent populations
were the under classes of most towns and cities
and here in Exeter, the West Quarter was
mainly where they lived.

As Todd Gray writes in this book, history
records very little of the lives of the poor and
this excellent little book goes some way to put
the matter right.

I heartily recommend this book as a very
good read.

THE RIGHT WORSHIPFUL THE MAYOR OF EXETER
Councillor Granville Baldwin

INTRODUCTION

In the winter of 1854 the population of Exeter was unsettled by serious public disorder prompted by the high price of bread. Twenty-six individuals, aged between thirteen and nineteen, were arrested for rioting on the 9th of January and put on trial ten weeks later on March 17th. Many worked as common labourers and two were described as 'gatherers' of bones and cinders. In the crowded courtroom at Rougemont Castle the judge declared that one individual, Charles Tuckett a shoe-maker aged nineteen, should receive what he considered what was not a hard punishment but one which would be 'a warning in this town': he was sentenced to imprisonment for nine months with hard labour.

Four days after the trial *The Western Luminary and Family Newspaper for Devon, Cornwall, Somerset and Dorset,*[1] a newspaper based in Post Office Street, Exeter, began a series of investigative reports into the state of the city's poor. They were published in ten sections[2] from March 21st to June 13th and written by an unidentified writer who referred to himself as a journalist and used the *nom de plume* 'A White Slave'. It appears that the articles were written only days before they were published. The writer observed that the public was fascinated to read about the poor in novels and thought that they should be equally interested to learn about them from real life.

The reports were obviously intended to coincide with the trial and may have been an attempt not merely to be topical but to influence public opinion. The essence of the reports was that the city had many residents who deserved public assistance because they were the 'virtuous' poor in contrast with those who were intentionally idle. The writer stressed it was in the general interest to have the poor contribute to society rather than merely receive public funds: they were more useful as wage earners than as charity recipients. The reports have a high moral tone; he alluded to the sense of moral shame, even of guilt, in being poor, noted the merits of the Protestant Bible and referred to the ministrations of the Church of England. Even so, he denigrated the Roman Catholic faith, which although not unusual in Exeter in the 1850s was particularly relevant given a significant number of the individuals he met were from Ireland.

Rival local newspapers were harsher in their treatment of the poor: *The Exeter and Plymouth Gazette*, the leading Conservative paper, thought they were ungrateful and *The Western Times* considered the poor should be educated in the merits of the free market.[3] Immediately following the riots *The Western Luminary* explored the reasons for the public disorder and while it considered bread shortages had been the declared reason for the French Revolution it questioned to what extent domestic politics there, and recently in Exeter, was the real cause. It suggested that journalists from rival newspapers should re-examine whether they contributed to an atmosphere of civil unrest. The paper also reported that the male rioters were 'more like idle vagabonds than anything else' and of a group of other women questioned it suggested that they 'even after these few days' prison discipline had the marks of dissipation legibly sculptured in their faces, one only of them appeared to be a decent-looking woman.'

But the tone changed after the trial. *The Western Luminary* stressed through these reports that it was the responsibility of Exeter's middle classes to strive to understand the nature of poverty in their city rather than merely condemn it. The issue of how society should best help the poor was a recurring concern in Exeter[4] as with all other cities, towns and villages.

The West Quarter received particular attention and the journalist visited many buildings which were either later removed as part of Exeter's slum clearance[5] or through bombing in the Second World War. The anonymous writer remarked that the West Quarter had previously been notorious for harbouring criminals but was, in his opinion, greatly changed. The living conditions which he found were desperate and the lives of those in them wretched. Among those he described living in Sherman's Court, a collection of houses which were located near the West Gate, were the Sullivan family. The husband and wife shared one room with their five children. Their income was derived from various sources including through matches being sold by their children, who most probably looked similar to the children depicted on the cover of this book. The Sullivan's poverty was matched by those he subsequently met in spite of extraordinary efforts on the part of some to improve their positions: one woman walked every morning to Stoke Canon to work in the mills there. Not surprisingly, the journalist encountered people who suffered from physical and mental illness.

The writer reflected public concerns about the cleanliness of the poor and its corresponding effect on the spread of infectious disease. He continually noted their efforts to maintain high standards of hygiene in spite of their poverty. This was of particular public concern given that Exeter, like many other Victorian cities, had recently suffered from cholera. The accounts noted some of the poor were still haunted by memories of the disease in 1832 when more than 400 people died in Exeter.[6] The writer approached the issue by noting there was a public duty to point out any causes for concern and praised the mayor for his efforts to improve public health by expelling livestock from the city: he noted that 400 pigs were forced from their quarters in the yards of 'respectable' people in the city across Exe Bridge. There was also concern about the number of children who had died of disease and the journalist questioned whether the native and immigrant populations had different rates of mortality.

The writer also visited the workhouse, an extraordinary building erected in the late 1690s which was situated on Heavitree Road. A fragment survives as part of the complex of buildings of the Royal Devon & Exeter Healthcare NHS Trust. The workhouse was run by the Corporation of the Poor, a poor law union with jurisdiction for some nineteen parishes and three precincts, administered by the mayor, eight city magistrates and forty guardians. In the first half of the nineteenth century there were continual frictions between the city authorities and the Corporation of the Poor and from the 1830s there were disagreements with central government then much concerned with reforming the provision of the poor in Exeter as with the rest of the country.[7]

'The White Slave' was given a tour of the

building in which he was shown the efforts made to make the inhabitants productive and explained the care that was taken of them. The journalist approved of much of what he saw with some exceptions including that married paupers were not allowed to remain together at the workhouse.

One of his most astonishing descriptions is of Dahlia Graham, a woman of 93 who was first sighted seated in a cane chair with her head covered with a brightly coloured scarf. He recounted her life history: she had been kidnapped from Africa as a child, sold into slavery, shipped to Africa and then released upon the abolition of slavery in the British Dominions in 1833. In the writer's opinion Miss Graham 'rejoiced' in her accommodation at the workhouse and in the care she received there: she was 'somewhat eloquent', 'exceedingly happy' and 'very grateful'. Also, he considered that Miss Graham was very fortunate in that she would have had a less happy life had she been left undisturbed in Africa. The Census of 1851 listed Delia Graham as employed as a General Upper Servant in a house in Hill's Court Road, later called Pennsylvania Road. Another source, *The Exeter Journal and Almanack*, shows the house was known as Rose Cottage, near the lower corner with West Avenue. The house retains its name.

Miss Graham was listed in the census as having been born in Senegal and the head of the household was Mrs Harriet Louisa Wardrobe, a widow aged 76. According to *The Western Luminary* journalist the Wardrobe family had bought the young girl from the slave-dealer after whom she had been named. Presumably in 1833 the former slave was employed as a servant by the Wardrobe family for the ensuing twenty years or so until sometime between 1851 and 1854 when, after a lifetime of service as a slave and then as a paid servant, Miss Graham was rewarded by being sent to the Exeter

Workhouse. Mrs Wardrobe died shortly afterwards in 1856.[8]

These investigations into the poorest members of society are a boon to the historian: the poor generated much less documentary evidence than their fellow wealthier citizens. Fortunately there is a stark difference between the lives of these Victorians with the vast majority of those who live in Exeter today. Even so, in the first years of the new millennium the reports are a useful reminder of society's continuing dilemma of how best to look after those not able to do so themselves. The nineteenth-century journalist noted 'poverty and vice are a sorry scene, but poverty and virtue are a scene on which an angel might pause in its flight to linger'. Many of these poor people lived in the Elizabethan ramshackle buildings for which the city was known, epitomised today by The House That Moved, and which countless visitors daily admire and photograph. The history of these buildings lies not only in their architectural merits but also in considering the lives of some of those remembered here in these pages.

1   *The Alfred* was inorporated in 1831.

2   Some of the reports have not been reprinted including accounts of the effects of heavy traffic on Coombe Street, of the erection of model houses, and of the county gaol.

3   Robert Newton, *Victorian Exeter, 1837-1914* (Leicester, 1968), 152-3.

4   See Wallace T. MacCaffrey, *Exeter, 1540-1640* (Cambridge USA, 1975 EDN), 110-111, 114-115; W.B. Stephens, *Seventeenth-Century Exeter* (Exeter, 1958), 13-14, 147-8; Robert Newton, *Eighteenth-Century Exeter* (Exeter, 1984), 159-61; Newton, *Victorian Exeter*; W.J.Forsythe, 'Paupers and Policy Makers in Exeter, 1830 - 1900', *Transactions of the Devonshire Association*, 117(1985), 151-60.

5   W.G. Hoskins, *2000 Years in Exeter* (Exeter, 1960), 130.

6   Thomas Shapter, *The History of the Cholera in Exeter in 1832* (1849).

7   Forsythe, 'Paupers'.

8   She was buried on 8 July 1856: Devon Record Office, Parish Register of St David's, Exeter.

AN HOUR
WITH THE EXETER
POOR, OR THE
DEFORMED
TRANSFORMED

The truly philanthropic man always contemplates the condition of the poor by which he is surrounded with the deepest interest - sometimes with feelings of hope mingled with despair. Poverty and vice are a sorry scene; but poverty and virtue are a scene on which an angel might pause in its flight to linger. It is to be feared that too many instances of the former abound in this city as well as elsewhere, and when we consider that hunger and squalor have many thorns, we shall be slow to pronounce a judgement of great severity even upon those who are the occupants of viscous and cheerless abodes - for to estimate truly their moral guilt we must first ascertain what circumstances brought them to so degrading a condition.

The case of virtuous poverty needs *no* apology; it is a sight of a noble character; it is a triumph that appeals to our nobler instincts and enlists the sympathies of our noblest facilities. Thanks to the Bible, the open Bible of the Protestant, and its legitimate expounders there are many such cases to be met with in the city of Exeter, though it may happen that, on this occasion, we may not give many examples.

The city of Exeter, like every other large place, has its dirty purlieus where the idle and the dissipated gather; its alleys and its dens where those abandoned creatures, whom society, by common consent, have shunned and cast forth as Cain-like vagabonds, stained with loathsome crimes, withered by loathsome disorders - men who cannot be touched without dishonour; women who cannot be countenanced without shame. But Christianity and the Press, destined to work a moral revolution in the earth, have poured forth floods of intelligence, and these 'dens' and the 'habitations of cruelty' are being destroyed, or lessened in the heinousness of their character. Time was when 'The Western Quarter' was a sound of dread; at its mention some ghastly idea of crime shot through the mind - nothing pleasant was associated with that name. But now 'The Western Quarter', though still the rendezvous of the Irish and the English poor, has little of its old horrors about its sound. 'The Western Quarter' is greatly transformed. The Church and the Press have melted down many of its rough-looking, crime-stained features, and now, in many parts, virtuous poverty hath supplanted dishonour, and industrious habits have superseded idle filth and rags.

The scenes are changed very much, but still enough of crime, and poverty, and sin, remain to awaken our warmest sympathies and to rouse to activity the slumbering efforts of a Christian laity.

Let us take the reader into one of the notorious haunts of 'The West Quarter'. Here it is, a stone throw from the quay - it is the well-known 'Sherman's Court'. According to tradition many an unholy thing has been committed in this notorious court. When the police formerly wanted a blood-stained scoundrel, or a felon polluted with every vice, they hunted this famous rendezvous for him, and, as we have heard, were often successful, - the character of this place, we are bound to say, is greatly altered. The court is a pile of what - to be romantic - we will call 'ruins'. They are held, as we are informed, by a Mrs Gorman, a very intelligent woman, who, to continue the vein of romance, has lately had the misfortune to lose a not very gallant husband, for whom she, after the most approved fashion, 'sighs and pines', and 'breaks her heart'. This Mrs Gorman sub-lets the ruins to those who are in want of something to shelter them from the elements - for to call the houses 'homes' would be, according to our taste, a perversion of the term - but the Irishman who calls the gate a door, and a field a bed, would consider these 'ruins' a kind of Celtic palace. Mrs Gorman has tried to get these houses, or some portion of them, 'licensed', but they are pronounced to be unfit for the purpose, a decision which Mrs Gorman thinks savours with injustice! *That's* her idea of things.

Now if the reader would wish to see the interior of some of these habitations, let him walk up stairs - the house is without number, but is situate about mid-way up the court, on the right-hand side, as you enter - and he will see no dirt, but grey, damp, walls, smelling of age or mildew, such as a civilized eye is not accustomed to. The stairs creak at the foot's pressure, and their elasticity facilitates your advancement. Enter this little room - it is the home of Mr Dimpsey, an Irishman, and his humble partner. The apartment is as clean as the circumstances will permit, - cleaner than you expect, and the good man is hard at work mat making. There are several new mats on the ground, and he says he will sell them to you from 1 shilling to 1 shilling 6 pence each. His rent, coals, and candles, cost about 4 shillings a week, and his earnings average about 12 shillings. He has been in this 'house' about four years, and has never had any sickness, and only known one or two cases of serious illness.

Let us descend - on the ground floor there is a family of Sullivans - 5 children, an aged father and mother. They are exceedingly robust, and the eldest is a young woman of 18, good looking, and somewhat remarkable for *embonpoint*, considering all things. They all live in one room (not very large) in which they are obliged to do every mortal thing that a house of 10 rooms would not be too large for. Mr Sullivan gets his living by selling sundry things, and 'jobs' while his children get a 'trifle' by vending matches, and so forth. They earn, collectively, 10 shillings a week, one shilling six pence of which is paid for rent. They were tempted to fly from the inhospitable shores of Ireland in 1844, but have never suffered so great privations as they have during the past winter. The wife, who is rather a pre-possessing woman and well-mannered, said 'I have suffered a great deal since I have been in England, but I have suffered honestly'. The whole family are attached to the 'ancient faith' but neither of them can read, except the father, and a little child who goes to the Roman Catholic school. They have a Catholic Prayer Book but no Bible. The poor woman told us that she much deplored her not being able to read, as did also her eldest daughter, and in answer to our question she said that 'Roger' her husband, had told her that between the Roman Catholic's and the Protestant's Bible, there was only 'one or two words difference'. She added that her priest, Mr Eccles, was very kind to her, and very frequently called upon her.

Across the road we find on the first-floor, a somewhat affecting sight. It is the house of Mrs Roche of Ireland; the husband is a labourer, and she has two children. He was driven from his country five years ago, just after the famine and cholera had decimated that unhappy country. He pays 1 shilling 6 pence a week rent, and earns about six shillings a week. Mrs Roche is sadly indisposed, and her infant lying in her somewhat wretched bed, looks as pale and as innocent as the snow-drop. The hapless mother seems exceedingly patient under her affliction, and informs her visitors that her priest is attentive and that a 'lady' is very kind to her.

From this cheerless cabin let us ascend some ragged stairs by sombre, and musty, foetid walls, the abode of Mr Richard Ivey. He is a venerable and viceless looking man - aged 73. He has a wife a good deal his junior, and who has a double qualification, being not only a sleeping but a 'working partner'. He is a native of Helston, in Cornwall, and now lives on a 'pension' of 1 shilling a day. He has, however, resided in this city for nearly 20 years; and now complains very loudly of the high price of bread. His own pittance is materially assisted by his 'working partner' who walks to Stoke [Canon] nearly every day and earns from six pence to nine pence per day in the mills there! This is an example that might be followed with advantage by many who are much younger. Mrs Ivey is the picture of health and appears as fresh as a 'rose in June'.

Patrick Calbert, a regular 'Paddy', lives at 'No. 3'. He thinks he is about thirty, and tells you with great gusto that he married his present wife (10 years ago) who is *only* sixty (!) when he was fifteen. He is the father of three children by his lovely countrywoman, two of whom are gathered to the grave, the third survives. He gets his living by selling tape, &c., 'by the basket' as he said. He gets about four shillings per week, and had fasted ever since five o'clock yesterday afternoon! He says that his countrymen were dying as fast as they could five years ago in Ireland and he, to save his life, 'hooked it' and came over to England. He is attached to the ancient faith, but can't read. His father didn't give him any education and 'that is the way he did not like him'. We were very much interested in Pat's case and asked him how he managed to live on 4 shillings a week. So Pat reckoned up his various 'courses'. They were: two meals a day consisting of a half a quartern loaf 4½ pence (between three persons), a fish 2d, fat 1½ pence, tea ¾ pence, sugar 1 penny, equal to 9¾ pence per day or 5 shillings 8¼ pence per week, and my wife, says Paddy, 'finds the firing'. So Paddy earned 4 shillings a week and lived upon 5 shillings 8¼ pence besides 'firing'. Pat had a drap o' beer sometimes, and then he never had any meal for the day. He is also attached to the religion of the Pope and his 'Praste' is a due attendant at his 'house'. Pat goes to church, and his priest tells him what is true and what is false, what right and what wrong: Pat knows there is a Heaven, but can't say much about Hell. Thinks his soul is his body, but is not learned enough to discuss the subject. If he thought he were going to die, he should send for the 'praste'. We recollect supping at an old friend's house, in the south of France one evening, when our friend, who was the principal merchant in the place, told us precisely the same thing respecting an aged mother, then about 85 years of age; he should call in the priest, he said, and he would make it all right for her when she was going to be gathered to her fathers! So the Creed is the same in France - the case we allude to took place in the days of Louis Phillippe, and the tone may now be somewhat altered - and in England, among merchant princes and humble vagrants.

Mr Wills occupies 2 rooms in the same court; he is a broom maker, has two children; earns about 6 shillings a week, and pays 1 shilling 6 pence a week rent. Missus seldom goes to church, nor does her husband; she can't read very well. He can read but little; has a Protestant's Bible in the house, but seldom looks in it; her children, she says, often suffer much from hunger; and their countenances confirm the statement.

William Smith, in the next house, is a sweep; his wife a nice-looking woman, the mother of six children, one of whom is a deplorable cripple. They have endured great privations of late. The husband is a sweep, never drinks, but doesn't earn more than 6d a day. 'No shambles' had been in her house for the last six weeks. Was obliged to pledge her child's frock today to get some victuals with. Mrs Smith appears a well-mannered person, neatly dressed and very clean - though her cabin wore the same rickety, dingy, and unwholesome aspect as the others, a circumstance inseparable from the system and the poverty by which she is surrounded.

Up at the top of this house we found a very curious, a very interesting, and perhaps, a very melancholy case. On the one side dwells an honest-looking and elderly boot and shoemaker; on the other, a lady about 60 years of age - a spinster. She saluted us very warmly; and brought out in her hand a neatly bound volume of Moore's works, as well as we could discover. She read down, in a very hasty manner, the 'dedication'; and said that it had reference to some vast property (upwards of £240,000,000) to which she was entitled; but which a great many gentlemen, whose names she mentioned, of this county, had kept, she said, from her. She called herself 'Mary Bryant Victoria' and presented to us a well-written form of an order to this effect 'pay Queen Victoria two million pounds. (signed)'.

She repeatedly assured us that she was the victim of intrigue, and the names of a great number of fire offices were mixed up in it. Miss Bryant urgently solicited our interference and appealed to us if she were not talking like a sensible woman. The reader will see that there was some strange hallucination here; that there was some mental alienation. We expressed our belief to that effect, but the neighbours would not listen to such a notion, and gave the ambitious lady an excellent character for her good disposition and good character, except when excited. We cannot, however, believe that she is a proper person to be left alone, without some kind of supervision; if she has any friends whose eyes may see this, we hope they will do their duty towards her, and so prevent what may otherwise befall her - some lamentable catastrophe.

We learn from Mrs Gorman that Miss Bryant was well connected, but that her last relative died at Torquay six months since, when the eccentric lady was left 7 shillings per week, on which she now subsists. We have no doubt that Miss B. was *tres joli femme* when younger, and, even now, she appears to have sufficient charms to win the affections of the honest cobbler, whose domestic concerns she attends to with great regularity, attention and generosity. She has lived in this 'cabin' during the past ten years and appears exceedingly healthy (physically). This house was ventilated by means of large vacant window place; at the top, which we fancied a dangerous aperture, considering who lived within a foot of it.

This, then, gentle reader, is about the 'sum and substance' which we saw in the course of Wednesday afternoon at Sherman's Court, and we may add that although the houses wore a desolate appearance, being exceedingly grey, and damp, and ragged; though as many as seven or eight in a family lived, and did all their work, in one room; though the furniture was of the humblest description, and exceeding scant and drear; though it was dingy and dismal with age and use; there was the stamp of honest industry about the *tout ensemble*. Fancy a man and his wife and five children living upon 10 shillings a week, in one room, about 12 feet square! Fancy the thousand wants of that family being all attended to in that hovel! Fancy, at the same time, that the loaf of bread is at famine price, and the wonder will be that the oppressed Celt, exiled from home and his kindred, has not sunk into an irredeemable state of slothness and wretchedness - in a word that he is not a moral and material wreck - but no, he enjoys domestic happiness, and his wife and children are healthy, and cheerful, and well-behaved!

We cannot conclude this notice without paying a tribute of praise to the Reverend F. Turner, who, it would appear from some statements made on the occasion, has been exceedingly active in his parish in ministering to the varied necessities of its poor by whom, we were told, the reverend gentleman is often besieged - besieged by persons driven to his doors by the uncompromising thorn of hunger.

It is due, however, to the visited to state that the whole of the inhabitants received us with the most cordial greetings, were exceedingly frank and respectful, and had a good idea of the object of our mission, so that while they were taken by 'surprise' having nothing shameful to conceal, they opened the virtuous breast of honest poverty for the severest criticism, and bowed us out without presuming to whisper for alms - the crying sin of the children of the Sacred Island.

THE CONDITION
OF THE POOR
OF EXETER,
MORTALITY AMONG
THEIR CHILDREN

To visit the haunts of criminals, to plunge
into the *foci* of fever, to tread the creaking
boards of tattering ruins, and to gaze upon
sickly and sombre walls, are by no means
pleasant occupations for the Journalist; but
if the Clergyman goes among the disease
and squalor for the love he bears to the
victims; if the Physician dares confront
grim Death himself in his own province
and battle with him, to pluck his patient
from his terrible grasp, merely from cold
duty, or to win another triumph for that
science of which he is the exponent; if
some delicate lady can rise from the elegant

repose of her gorgeous couch, and go forth from a pure and fragrant atmosphere to the abode of pestilence and breathe the poisoned and fevered breath of the dying man or woman (in the last convulsive agonies of death) whose sickness she would allay, and whose pillow she would soften, what a miserable, stunted and withered moral courage the Journalist have, who would refuse to execute a mission to which he is invited, because the scenery is sombre and dismal, and the objects pallid and sickly, and flying to the winds in rags and tatters? It is enough that duty calls him, and, like the good soldier, he must obey. But, if we have visited some of the darker spots of our city - we have darker yet to see - it is not to conceal the facts in our own bosom, but to place them before the public, in order that they may have a proper conception of the element by which they are surrounded, and if need be, to endeavour to refine, and cultivate it. And here let us premise that if our remarks awaken curiosity only, they will have fallen very far short of what they were intended to accomplish. The facts are narrated to show men the religious, moral, and social conditions of the poor of the places mentioned, and who will dare say that he is not interested in the condition of the poor? Train your poor to habits of economy, temperance, and self-respect, and you will destroy much of the anarchical element which pervades the body politic; not only so, but you will lessen simultaneously, the poor rates, and the bill of mortality. We may build up barricades between ourselves and them, and refuse to gaze upon their sinister features, but nothing is more certain than that the invisible hand of retribution will punish us for such unfeeling and unenlightened conduct. Cut the poor off from the soft civilities of life, banish them into grey under-ground cellars, shaded by the frosty summits of an ungenerous opulence, and you debase them tenfold, you develop all their brute propensities, and they feel as if there is no bond of brotherhood between them and you, but visit them when sickness overtakes them, when fortunes frowns upon them, and you elevate their thoughts, refine their affections, and win their admiration; not only so, but you thrown an aegis round yourselves. You cannot allow fever to carry off the husband without pauperising the family, and if the cholera sweeps away the poor by scores it picks off the rich by units. Let a pestilence break out in a hamlet, or a city, and who will dare say, 'I am safe?' It may manifest itself, first, in the lowest den in the city, but the seeds of death will radiate far and wide, and the sigh of the widow, in the house of penury, will be answered by the note of mourning in the mansion of the rich! And why should it not be so? Are not the poor, men and women, degenerate transcripts of God's image, and does not Lazarus, the beggar, repose in the bosom of Abraham, while the gorgeously arrayed rich man - where is he?

But let us lift the veil and exhibit the scenery. Here is Water Lane, the 'West Quarter'. The exterior of the house before us is very wretched, and its approach is dismal. It has the appearance of a dissolute den. Let us walk up stairs. It is ghastly, it looks *vicious*, but it may not be so. On the first floor lives one Vinnicombe. He is a very useful, but a very humble, member of society. He is employed by Mr Harris, the contractor for cleansing the streets; his occupation is to cleanse the drains, &c, a very loathsome but necessary occupation. He receives 10 shillings a week, wages, and pays 1 shilling 6 pence, rent. He appears to be a well-conducted man, has a wife and two children living - five have DIED! The place he considers is now tolerably healthy, but, last summer, the small pox raged very fatally here. He has lived in this locality 15 years, & thinks it quite transformed since the row of cottages opposite were pulled down. He called our attention to a most offensive gutter which runs down in the middle of the court, discharging itself into a sewer which leads from thence to the river. This gutter is frequently filled with the most offensive matters by dirty neighbours, and when the sun shines upon it by and bye, look out for the fever! This man's room is tolerably decent for such a house.

Up stairs is John Larkworthy, broom maker. He has lived there five or six months. He has a wife, and two children; earns about 7 shillings a week and pays 11 pence rent. This little cabin is a desolate and cheerless place, and the occupants look very wretched and stunted. We leave these ghastly places and visit

John Clarke's, just touching it. He is a quay labourer, was born in the court, and always enjoyed good health. Has had, by Mary, his wife, six children, four of whom are DEAD! two died from small pox, and two from consumption. He earns about 7 shillings a week and pays 11 pence out of it for his room, where they have lived about three years. Never knew so hard a winter as the last winter was. This house used to be occupied, Mrs C. tells us, by most desperate characters, but now is as different as 'light from darkness'. She complains very much of the gutter mentioned above.

James Willis, broom maker, lives next door; he has a wife and three children living, two have DIED! died of the small pox in this locality; pays 1 shilling 6 pence a week rent, and earns about 6 shillings a week; a little boy gets 2 shillings 6 pence a week at the mill. The rooms (three) are a picture of cleanliness, and so are the family - an example of poverty and neatness.

George Backeller lives just long side of the above; is also a quay porter. Has a wife and five children all living; gives 1 shilling a week for two rooms; met with a misfortune sometime ago, and has not earned 5 shillings since Christmas; has been sustained by the hand of public charity.

The next house here is anything but an inviting place. Let us enter it - somebody lives here; this is the residence of Charles Bragg, a labourer; works at the reservoir; has two rooms for which he pays 1 shilling 2 pence a week; has a wife and one child living - one child has DIED. The rooms are creditably kept, and the occupants look healthy.

Up stairs resides Mr John Ralton, an

aged mason, with his wife, who has reached the venerable age of threescore and ten. They have lived here 10 years, and have been healthy during the whole of that time. This old lady is very intelligent, and tells us some awful tales about the sad havoc made by cholera in the neighbourhood, in 1832. In fact, that appears to be a date that is deeply sculptured in the memories of all the inhabitants in the locality. She speaks very highly of the Reverend Mr Lee, who constantly visits her. She pays 1 shilling a week rent, and her husband, who goes to work in the country, sends her about 2s 6d a week more. Neither she nor her husband can read: but the room and furniture are clean and decent. She has lost a daughter lately, by DEATH!

The back part of these houses is washed by the river.

Now we are in Thomas' s Court, Frog

Lane. We were told that it was a heap of ruins and filth: it is no such thing - that was a libel. The people are poor; but, so far as we could find, respectably conducted.

The first house we enter is the abode of Mr Edward Hockin, a carpenter. He and his wife are very nice-looking, but elderly, people. He is 64, and his partner 69, years of age. He complains of having more appetite than food, and has not earned 5 shillings a week since Christmas. Mrs Hockin says that she used to work at Mr Worthy's factory, where she used to get good wages, and she (like many others) deplores that the factory is closed. Mr Hockin has applied for some relief, but the authorities refuse him, unless he goes into the Union-house. From this step his soul seems to revolt with the pride of an Englishman, the venerable couple appear determined to perish from hunger, before accepting such a miserable and heartless alternative, which cannot be defended upon any Christian principle, whatever 'expediency' may say.

The house of Mr Sprague is hardly so orderly, but there was nothing to complain of in a sanitary point of view, that we could observe. He is a labourer and earns 12 shillings a week; has a wife and four children living - one is DEAD!

Let us now go into Hick's Court, in the island. It is represented as a miserably dissolute place; but the representation is wholly false. The first house we enter is that of Mr Russell, a labourer, at the foundry. There is nothing to remark here, except an absence of disorder.

Here lives Mr Martin, next door to Mr Russell; he is a sawyer, has a wife and five children living; four children have been swept away by DEATH! They have lived here a great many years. The surviving children look healthy. The inhabitants here complain of nothing, except a very offensive small which proceeds from some sewerage pipes leading from the backs of houses in Fore Street, which they say is intolerable, at times. The river runs along, at the head of the Court, and a pump has been recently erected, so that water is obtainable on all occasions. We are told that the sewerage of this court is good, and all offensive matter is carried off by the river, which is now running very rapidly.

We leave the island and come back to Ewing's Lane, a place that has long worn a very indifferent reputation, moreover, it is a place where cholera left many a fearful foot-print. The place is much changed in its aspect of late years, and we observe one or two nice houses are erected here; and 'as virtue advances, vice recedes'.

The first house we enter is that of Mrs Warren (a widow), 69 years of age, but as brisk as a butterfly. She informs us that she has lived in this street 50 years. She recollects, with dread, when the choleric pestilence decimated this street, 'particularly that part near the water,' in 1832. Fever has from time to time appeared here lately, and carried off a great many children - a circumstance which she thinks 'a very great blessing'.

Let us enter this passage - dark and loathsome, on the opposite - the 'water side'. The house is somewhat large, and if we might judge by the carve-work inside, has seen better days. On the left hand side you enter (downstairs) the room of one William Reed, a quay-labourer. He has had a wife and 3 children, two of whom have DIED! He has lived in this street 13 or 14 years; the small-pox reigned here 12 months ago, and carried off a great many children. They pay 1 shilling a week rent for one room. The husband earns not more than 2 shillings a week, being an invalid; but she earns 5 shillings a week at Mr Harris' mill. They have suffered much from hunger, during the past winter.

The next 'cabin' of this wretched-looking place is occupied by John Ward and his family. Look at the ensemble of this dreary room, and fancy it, if you can, the habitation of human beings, in the midst of what Mr Baron Martin is pleased to call, and with great truth, we have no doubt, a 'prosperous city'. John Ward is an Irishman, and his abode is so much like what one reads of respecting those in some parts of Galway, that we were tempted to ask him if he came from thence. His reply was no, but from Sligo. He has a wife and 3 or 4 little children. Everything in the 'cabin' has an air of dark and damp desolation - except his crockery ware, which was clean but scant - and the silence of the abode was gloomy and almost sepulchral. The fact was that the unhappy

Celt and his offspring were under the pressure of poverty and solitude in a strange land - very bitter things you may depend. The wife and children sat in silence in one part of the room - in another corner, heaped up in the shape of a section of a Roman tumulus, was a bed - that is to say some miserable straw covered by a more miserable piece of Hessian, dark and wretched - in a third corner was a similar bed, and in the fourth was poor Ward, looking with piteous down-cast eye upon a bale of rags in the middle of the room, which he had just thrown from his weary shoulder, having come off a journey of 20 miles. What was passing through his mind? It might well have been such a sentiment as this:

- Such, alas!
Are the illusions of this protens life,
All, all is false - through every
*   phasis still,*
'Tis shadowy and deceitful.

He had been driven from his famine-stricken and priest-ridden country in pursuit of bread, and here he was, after 7 years, a wretched pilgrim, a miserable bone and rag picker, in a strange land without even a priest to offer him the consolations of the ancient faith by which his mind might be nerved to surmount the bitterness of the present! 'I cannot read my Bible,' he said, and 'Mr Eccles never calls upon me, but it is no use to repine'. Unhappy Celt, Heaven protect thee!

Up stairs, on the next floor, lives Mrs E. Hill, a widow. She pays 1 shilling a week rent and has three persons living with her in the same room. She has wanted bread many times this winter, but her 'house' is clean. She has 'nothing to complain of, except poverty'.

At right angles, there, is John Pike, a poor fellow who has lately had a leg amputated, and is depending upon the efforts of his wife for subsistence. She earns 5 shillings a week at Countess Wear. The authorities have refused him any assistance unless he go into the Union-house, and there he positively refuses to go, for, said the poor fellow - 'my furniture would be sold, and how should I ever get it together again.' Furniture! Is it worth a crown? But that's his all; he refuses to be walled up in the workhouse, cold and cheerless as it is at best, with the censorship of the law of man over him, and the law of God defied and violated. Union-houses do very well for poor bachelors and dependent widowers, but don't think of winning the affection of married people by their cold and stately formality. We should think John Pike a fit object of charity, he having been prevented from work during the past eleven months. He speaks highly of Mr Cumming who might probably be able to say something respecting his deserts.

At the very top of this dingy and dreary dwelling-house lives a man, and his wife, and seven children in one little room. The husband is named John Collins, an Irishman; the eldest child is fifteen years of age, and the youngest hangs at her mother's breast. The condition of this family is very wretched. The poor woman, who is of prepossessing manner, told us that she had been driven here from Ireland 5 years ago. The little cabin was decorated by a number of fine-looking children, while the wife sat by the side of a bark-fire. There appeared to be no comfort in the room which seemed almost destitute of everything in the shape of furniture. There was a fine youth lying down on a straw bed by the side of the room, suffering from fever, as the mother said: he appeared wan and languid, whilst at times there stood upon his cheek a kind of hectic blush. The window of the garret was opened and he seemed to say:

Blow on me, wind! I faint with heat,
 O bring
Delicious water from the deepest spring

Cheer me, my friends! with looks of
 kindness cheer;
Whisper a word of comfort in mine ear.

He had been in this condition, his mother said, five weeks. Her husband earned his living by going in the country with a basket. He did not get 10 shillings a week; and she had fasted all that day, and had no stockings on her feet (Wednesday last). She paid 9 pence a week rent for her room. Her priest, Mr Eccles, she said, was very attentive to her, and a 'lady' was also very kind to her. She told us that although she had suffered so much here, she would rather live in England than in Ireland, where she fasted just two days, before she left that country. She added that Mr Cumming was exceedingly attentive to her son.

Thomas Henley, a labourer, also lives in this house; has a room and pays 1 shilling a week for it. He earns about 6 shillings a week, has one child living, and has lost another by DEATH! His apartment is tolerably clean.

William Reed (no relation to the Reed down stairs), also resides in this house. He works at the brick-field and gets 5 shillings a week, and his wife gets 1 shilling 6 pence a week. She used to work at Mr Worthy's, and regrets the factory is closed.

In this house there are no less than seven families, who number, collectively, about 40 persons, and it would not surprise any man if disease were enthroned there.

Lastly, what do these facts teach us? They teach us, that among the poor of these quarters there is much wretchedness, patience, industry, mixed up with suffering & ignorance, disease & death; they teach us, too, that the characters residing in these places are not so base as those who formerly lived in them; and that the sanitary condition of the localities is improved, but that there is room for still further improvements. These revelations also teach us that there is little or no knowledge among the people. Few of the parents or children can read, and as few go to church. What is the hope of such a population? They want a new creation; for it is a human desert seldom irrigated by the streams of living truth; it is a soil which the spirit of regeneration, we fear, has scarcely breathed into. With little moral development, when winter howls round their doors and hunger pinches them, what wonder if they are a source of annoyance, and their brute passions break forth, as they have done in the last winter. Finally, these facts teach us that the Church has not forgotten her duty among these poor people, but it may be that the laity has not stretched forth the hand of generosity so liberally as it should have done in order that her plans may be so fully carried out as she could wish them to be.

•

If we calculate the mortality among the children born in these houses, or of parents who have lived there any number of years, we shall find that it is very distressing. Of 57 children, born of parents now inhabiting these premises, 21 have died, or nearly *thirty seven per cent*; but, of 35 children who were probably born in those places, or of parents who have resided there some years, we find that no less than SIXTY PER CENT have been swept away by disease; and *this* is the proper basis for making the calculation, for the migratory

Irish children, have not been long enough in these abodes to be inoculated by the poisoned atmosphere to which the natives fall an early prey.

THE CONDITION OF THE EXETER POOR AND SANITARY CONDITIONS OF THE CITY

'And if I were asked what is the great want of English society, I would say that is the mingling of class with class; I would say in one word, that that want is the want of sympathy.'

DYING WORDS OF MR JUSTICE TALFOURD

We have already laid before the reader sundry facts relating to the condition of the poor located in various parts of the 'West Quarter' and in a portion of the 'Island' and though there was sufficient ignorance and misery in those parts of our city, though there was sufficient poverty and pain to make one weep, the state of the inhabitants of those places - confessedly among the worst parts of our city - is incomparably beyond the condition of the very poor in most other large towns, both in a moral and sanitary point of view. Indeed, the terrible accounts which we received of those portions of our city induced us to go and witness for ourselves, in order that we might see if things were not exaggerated. From all that we have seen in the 'West Quarter' we should say that since the day when the present excellent Chief Magistrate of this city, John Daw, esq., caused a thorough investigation to be made into the sanitary state of our town, when upwards of 400 pigs made their exit from various respectable abodes in our city, and walked over the bridge, a marked improvement has taken place in the social habits of the poor, no less than in their houses. Too much praise cannot be given to those gentlemen who have co-operated with Mr Daw in carrying out measures for the improvement of our town, as a place of residence; but still those who have read our previous remarks will find that, even now, there is much to be done before Exeter will be that *beau ideal* city which our Mayor promises it shall be. It is, however, due to all parties to say, that the 'West Quarter' is very far above anything which we could have expected to find, and those who have not seen it for the last four years would scarcely believe it to be the same place.

Still, it would be unwise and unfaithful of us, when cholera is making its approach in several large towns, to attempt to conceal anything which, if made known, would speedily be attended to, to the benefit of the town. It is by exposing nuisances, and getting them removed, that we prevent disease and its melancholy consequences; and it is too late to speak of the cause of disease when it has become developed, and is sweeping away its helpless victims by scores and hundreds. All accounts prove that to remove a cesspool, or to cleanse a sewer in times of sickness, is the very way to aggravate the evil which it is desired to destroy. Nor let it be supposed, if we point out anything which is said to be inimical to healthy morals or animal life, that our pen is swayed by the spirit of party, for in treating a subject of so great and grave importance as the health of a city, it would be to degrade it, immeasurably, to descend so low.

Apropos of this, let us speak a word or two respecting Mr Tanner's premises, at the foot of Fore Street Hill. We made diligent enquiry of the inhabitants about the very offensive smell which is said to come from Mr Tanner's manufacturing operations on these premises. The result of our enquiry was this: several said that the bad odour was not so intolerable now as it was 12 months ago; others said they could scarcely smell it; while others describe the stench as being unbearable at times, and one lady informed us that she was frequently ill from it - we give the simple statements as we had them, and the reader must come to his own conclusion. We may observe, however, that if there by any odour from this manufactory which is inimical to human health, the locality in which it is being low, will, particularly in the summer season, increase its evil influence.

For the present we will leave the 'West Quarter' and take the reader to the head of the large parish of St Sidwell, where rumour has told strange tales of late, respecting the deaths of several persons. But rumour, with its thousand tongues, is often a false-speaker, and so it has proved in this instance. It was reported to us that several cases of typhus fever had occurred in some houses in 'Prospect Cottages'; while others stated that the parties died of starvation. We repaired thither, instantly, determined to see if either version of the case was correct. The exterior of these cottages is clean, but somewhat poor. We knocked at the house of the widow of one of the deceased persons, but no one was home, except four or five *little orphans* -a term of unequalled meaning in their case, you may be sure.

We then called at No. 3, the house of Mr Richard Greenway, a labourer, whose wife, in reply to our questions, told us that no fever had ever been in the place since she had lived in it; that four persons had died there within the past few days; a Mrs King, of 'a seizure', her husband of 'asthma' (both very old); a Mr Lazarus, an ashes-picker, also very elderly; and, lastly, -

a poor man, a labourer, named, as we understood, Aplin.

Now, the particulars of this case are very affecting and certainly (though by no means uncommon we fear, both here, and in every other town), ought not to be unrecorded. The pen of the novelist graphically describes a purely fictitious character, and we linger with patience and interest over many a page, and allow our sympathies to be enlisted in the cause of the creation of the fancy, why, then, should the uncoloured picture of reality fail to awaken our most humane feelings or command our sincerest attention?

Listen, then, to no dreamy, but a substantial tale of woe. Aplin is a labourer, as we have said. Last Thursday week he was at his work, was taken ill, grew worse, lingered on with all the sufferings which accompany inflammation of the lungs, and died - perished miserably - on the following Monday. Our informant tells us that she attended him during his illness and death, and she avers that he had nothing to eat - there was nothing in the house for him to eat - except a piece of *dry bread* and some *cold water* - from the Saturday till the hour he passed from this to the immediate presence of his Maker! Happy release from pain and poverty! The dry bread was purchased, not at the price of her honour - but at the price of his wife's comfort, might have been at the price of her life - she took off her undress, chemise, and all, and pawned it for a morsel of bread for her famishing children! From that night till Monday, when the poor man with bloodless cheek and throbless heart was surrounded by orphans and widow, no food was brought into his house, until the neighbours sent them in some bread. The man had no parochial relief, we were told - but was buried at the expense of the public, and, since his death, the widow and his children have had some parochial aid.

Today (Wednesday last), the widow was out to half-a-day's work - precious antidote to a painful bereavement - while her children - aged from 4 month's to 6 years, take care of themselves, in their wretched and fatherless home. The picture is unvarnished, ought it to be buried, like the cottage in which the poor fellow died. We have nothing to add, but that being commissioned by a lady who feels an interest in the condition of the poor to distribute 'tickets' among the most deserving, we left an order and retired from the heart-aching scene. (We have enquired at the proper quarter respecting this case, and find that our information, as to the parochial relief, is strictly correct.)

From this place we proceeded to examine several other courts up in the same neighbourhood, but found nothing particular whereof to complain. Thence, we diverged to Lion's Holt, at the foot of the hill, beautifully surmounted by the Revered Mr Carlyon's church (St James). The hand of improvement is also visible here. The reader will recollect that last Christmas twelve months', a heavy flood came down here, and washed away the foundations of the old and somewhat corrupt shades which had long stood there - the occupants fled, and now the old ruins are being taken down, and new houses erected instead.

Lastly, we remark, that in the neighbourhood of St Sidwell's, a very considerable number of dirty and ragged children spend the Sabbath in the most desecrating manner - the day seems quite secularised by them, and we are informed by them that they don't go to Church 'because they have no clothes'. Who will gather these little stony-hearted

Ishmaelites together, and set them in the path of duty? The Church would willingly do it - she is doing it so far as her means will admit - but the Church cannot do everything she could desire. The Church is expected to do more than is possible - she listens with attention to every suffering, and records with faithfulness every sigh that reaches her; she compassionates the distresses of every family, and lingers with sympathetic tenderness to the tale of dejected humanity where ever she may hear it; but if we fetter her benevolent action, by too great parsimony, or indifference to her just claims, how can we expect her to win these moral and spiritual triumphs among the hardened occupants of stony-streets and crowded courts?

THE EXETER
WORKHOUSE –
ITS INMATES, THEIR
OCCUPATIONS
AND TREATMENT

The Exeter Workhouse is not a Unionhouse, either in the popular acceptation of legal significance of that term - still less has it those dismal features which properly belong to the cold and cheerless Unions studded over the land by the consent of your 'expediency' men. The Exeter Workhouse is a palace compared to the Bastille-looking buildings which spring up under the shadow of Wm 4, chap. 76, both internally and externally, though the exteriors of some of the Unions sadly belie their interiors. The Union-house frowns down upon you, generally, while, internally, its massive doors, swinging upon massive hinges, remind you of some romantic tale of feudal castles - or, worse still, dungeons! The Exeter Workhouse has no such severity - tall elms spread their green foliage over you as you walk towards its portals; while the officials have more the air of mild rulers than legal task-masters.

The Exeter Workhouse was incorporated by Act of Parliament, in the year of grace 1697 or 1698, in the reign of William the 3rd, and the first mentioned Act has little or nothing to do with it except that the Government audit the accounts - that was for the union of parishes and the disunion of married people - a flagrant piece of legislation, quite in character with the latitudinarian spirit of the age. This establishment owes its origin to some great benefactors who are long since assimilated with the dust; and by the revenues from their gifts, and rates levied upon the citizens it is supported. It receives an income from various estates and houses, &c, of about £280 annually, and the last year's rates amounted to £8,125. For these sums we have several hundred of our poor well provided for, and schools maintained, and a hospital in an efficient state, we hope. The management is vested in the hands of a number of gentlemen (40) and the executive department is considered very good.

As a great deal has lately been said respecting the poor, and the condition in which the Vagrant's ward was in a short time ago, we accepted an invitation from a gentleman to look through the whole of the establishment, and now lay some account of it before our readers.

The vagrant's ward has been rendered immortal by the pathetic and somewhat disgusting tale of a girl of abandoned character, named Elizabeth Collins. Let us go into this ward; it is on the right hand, just as you enter the gateway. It is a room of considerable area, and well ventilated. There are eight beds in it, of the simplest character, four on each side, each bed being separated from the other by a piece of wood, which any person standing at any side of the room might see every occupant at one view. The beds are of straw, and the rugs coarse, but clean. The room has no furniture except a deal table and chair; but it smells fresh, and fully justified the remarks made respecting it by Mr W. Hooper, a few days ago.

On a few steps is the stone yard, adjacent to which is a shed where the men work in rainy weather.

Retracing our steps, and passing the foot of the ample and neatly-kept garden in front of the house is another vagrant's ward for males; it is much the same as the one just noticed. Adjoining this is the Oakum-room. Here several men are frequently employed in preparing yarn for to be converted into oakum. Now, however, there is only one man employed, and he appears to be somewhat deficient in mental power. He said he had been here only 12 months; that he could prepare 10 bundles of yarn (10 lbs weight) in a day, for the women to pick in the House. The process which the yarn underwent, in his hands, was simple. He had a large block of wood placed in the middle of the room, and putting the bundle of yarn on its top struck it with a mallet until he bruised it sufficiently, thus enabling the women to pick it into oakum much more easily. We have only to add that the operator had his little finger decorated with a ring - mosaic gold, mayhap - rather smart for a pauper, certainly! The next apartments were occupied by the Porter.

The Bath-room, on the left-hand side passing up towards the main building, has two baths, and, by a complete mechanical contrivance, hot and cold water is poured into them; the cisterns (two) are just up over the baths. This apartment is very clean, and two women were, at the time we visited it, repairing rugs.

The Receiving-ward has five beds, two of which were, at the moment we entered it, occupied by men from the lower parts of this city, and who were in so filthy a condition when brought to the House that they could not even be washed! But the glorious sun shines upon their rugged features, and soon they'll have the luxury of a bath, and then they will, probably, be admitted into other society.

The Chapel is entered at the centre of the pile of buildings at the top of the garden. It is a fine, lofty, comfortable-looking place, well ventilated - a place where we might well feel the spirit of devotion. The Chaplain, the Reverend Mr Bell, whose salary, we are sorry to hear, has been reduced - but the people fancy that clergymen can live by the air - 'thin air' - preaches twice every Sunday, besides performing service other times during the week, and visiting the wards Wednesday and Saturdays.

The Visiting-room is much improved of late years - it is used for the purpose of examining paupers in, ere they are 'adopted' - it is clean, airy and comfortable.

The Girl's School-room upstairs is a very spacious room, has a splendid view, and is well aired. There are about 26 girls taught in it at the present time, varying from two to 12 years of age. They are divided into three classes, according to their age, acquirements, &c. The room is adorned with appropriate maps. The children are dressed neatly and appropriately. They look - all of them - very healthy and spirited - nay, they brought to one's mind the beautiful picture of the children whom with Daniel were fed with pulse - they were so fair to look upon. Some of the writing of the children of the first-class was highly creditable to the children and to their mistresses, while the 'copy-slip' was of the right tone - 'Religion is the foundation of Peace' - what could be more appropriate?

The Women's Oakum-rooms are at the top of the House. There are from six to ten persons generally employed in this department, but on Wednesday last there were only four. They pick, respectively, about 2 lbs of oakum a day; and when a good batch is done, the superintendent, an inmate, rolls it up in large globe-like forms, and has them disposed of at 24s or 25s per cwt.

The Work-house is another place where all is activity - there were about 12 persons - women - busy at work; some knitting, some sewing - making garments &c for the inmates - all under the keen eye of Mrs Mason. The room is clean and cheerful, so are the people.

The Girl's Sleeping-ward is a very long room, upwards of 100 feet we should guess. It contains several windows, and 17 beds - all on iron steads. The beds are of flock, on each bed is a sheet, above that is another, then a blanket, then a rug; all appeared clean, and the room wholesome; at one end of this room a great number of children stay during a portion of the day. The aspect is a southern one, and the inmates look healthy.

The Aged-women's-ward (below) has 13 beds occupied now by 14 persons: at one end, separated by a petition, is the Day-ward for the same parties. At the moment we entered they had congregated round the fireplace, and their appearance was somewhat grotesque. We approached and observed one old lady seated in a cane-wrought chair with considerable ease and dignity. She saluted us blandly, and we soon observed that she was of African blood. A novel sight in our Union-house! Around her head was bound a many-coloured kerchief, in that fantastic style that obtains in tropical climates. She was somewhat eloquent; exceedingly happy, and very grateful. She told us that her name was Dahlia Graham, given her by an English family, to whom she was sold by a slave-dealer in the West Indies, of that name. She was the eldest of four children, and was very young when placed in the bonds of captivity. From the hands of Mr Graham she passed to those of Mr Wardrobe, who was, when she was sold to him, a large plantation holder, but the policy of our governments towards the West India planters having beggared many, the Wardrobe family, have been sufferers, and Dahlia rejoices in her present happy position. Such are the mutations of sublunary things! Dahlia, kidnapped in Africa, endured the horrors of the middle passage, was sold into bondage in our colonies, and now at the patriarchal age of 93, she has a mansion to live in, gardens to live in, and the lieges of the Queen of England to minister to her wants! Fortunate Dahlia. How different an end to that which would, probably, have awaited her in her own country!

We pass on to notice a ward used by young married women with children, and we observe one or two children (on whose brows sat pale Consumption) - decaying away - like expiring lamps - shortly to slumber with the dead! The father is some vagabond Irishman who has deserted his offspring. The room is creditably kept, and the beds (15) are of the same nature as before described.

The Old Women's ward is a very pleasant one; here are the 'blind, and lame, and halt' and they do no work, beyond what they please. They go to bed when they like, and get up when it suits them; provided always that they are at rest by eight o'clock at night. The warm beams of Apollo were reanimating their worn-out frames, even as we looked upon them on their peaceful pillows. Honour to Exeter, for taking care of our venerable Mothers - who taught us first to lisp! Montgomery says in his World before the Flood, that

Woman was created with a smile of grace.

We dare say she was, and looked very captivating as Adam awoke from his sleep, and found her radiant with beauty and virtue by his side, but these Eves have no smile - they are

Deeply-ploughed by time and
ghastly pale with woe.

but as they are passing to that bourne whence no traveller returns, let us soothe their sorrows all we can, ere they depart from the Valley of the Shadow of Death, for they are mothers.

The Probationary-ward for women is a place where females are kept till they are purified; it is a small ward and used to be appropriated to vagrants before the one noticed was erected at the foot of the garden. This place, too, is clean and fresh.

The Day-room for young women who have led lives of dishonour is on the ground floor. They are placed, at night, in separate cells, each of which, however, is well-conditioned, and well-ventilated, except those on the right-hand which may be somewhat deficient of light, from the construction, or the lack of proper windows, - but this, we believe, is about to be altered. These cells used to be occupied by lunatics who were under the surveillance of paupers; but the system was considered defective, and an alteration was made. The friends of Miss Collins may be informed that that 'unfortunate' occupied 'number 17', one of the best cells of the whole 24. The beds in these places are of the same kind as those already described, and quite good enough for the bed of repentance.

Mrs Joselyn, the nurse, an agreeable, active woman, occupies a neat and unambitious room down-stairs. It has two windows, and can command two years where some of the inmates of the House take their airing.

The Nursery is also down stairs, and an old woman, in real nurse-fashion, toning the young brats (6) to something like obedience - she appeared somewhat 'fussy', we thought.

The Laundry looks into a Drying-yard. Here you see all the implements necessary for carrying on the business or profession of a laundress, and heaps of clothes - the room, however, is clean and as orderly as the mangling, &c, will admit.

A few steps onwards, and we see the Wash-house - 7 women are at the tubs, which are convenient to hot and cold water. The place is clean and airy, and the washer-women (5) were dressed in a lightish blue striped gown without 'flounces' and that sort of thing, of course. While here, one of the women, an intelligent but frail Eve, came up, and earnestly implored our conductor to intercede for her, to get her release. She had a sister at Plymouth, she said, who desired that she would come and live with her, until she could get some work. The gentleman interrorgorated her very closely as to her motives, and promised her that her case should be represented to the Visitors, but unless she could show some letter to him from her sister, that would satisfy them, her request could not be granted; she might also apply to the Committee of Nine. This applicant calls herself the mother of four children, and yet was never in the position of the English wife! A pregnant and humiliating fact! The gentleman to whom she applied might well be careful of his customer.

Now we enter upon the General-drying-ground in front of the Hospital and thence into that building. There was nothing to remark in the Hospital, except that the interior, like every other place which we saw, was clean and comfortable;

beds, linen and patients. There was no particular case here, except that two young women (one a very fine, open countenanced girl) were laid down with spinal complaints; and an old woman named Johanna Discombe, aged 93, of this city, was as brisk and jocose as a girl in her 'teens'.

It has now advanced towards dinner-hour, and we enter the Hall, in the main building. Here are about 120 persons dining off pea-soup; and 102 persons are in some different parts of the House, being prevented, from various causes, dining with the rest. Their etiquette is simple enough, and their dishes humble; the latter consisting of tin cups, while they carry their porridge to their mouth with a metal spoon. The men and boys are one side of the Mistress's table, and the women and girls the other. The dinner is commenced and finished with grace, sung aloud, and here, as in other parts of the establishment, the greatest harmony and decorum prevailed. We should not omit to mention that very few able-bodied men were present, a very important fact.

In the Little-children's ward there were beds for 21; the children were supervised by an elderly woman, and they appeared very healthy.

The Quiet-old-men's ward, upstairs, contains eight beds; their day-ward is on the same floor, divided by a partition. We pass hastily through one or two other wards, for old men, and come to the top of the House, to the Boy's ward, where there are 17 beds. The room smells wholesome, and the view is exceedingly cheerful.

Now we come to a very excellent part - the Married people's ward - somewhat of a novelty in this kind of House. It contains ten beds, properly partitioned off - very different from the indecent plan which once obtained, but as a gentleman remarked the law of decency was not so well developed formerly. This ward, in our eye, is an excellent feature, but it is very limited, and, perhaps, wisely so. There are only ten beds and one only is now occupied. We were told that old worn-out married couples are allowed the privilege mentioned; and this is very humane, but why was Hockin refused? Pike was living in adultery; but Hockin was not, and was old enough, surely, getting on for 70. We have ever protested against the system, which, would lift up its iron hoof against all natural and revealed religion, and would rather see our virtuous poor die in their cabins, humble as they may be, than submit to so degraded a law as that which would separate the husband from the wife? We ask, with impatience, where is the authority for so blasphemous a step? Is it written in Nature or spued forth by some

Demon? But, and don't let us be misunderstood, we think the authorities act wisely by not permitting lazy, vicious men and women, to have so great a luxury – no unreasonable punishment would be too heavy to inflict upon the idle and the dissipated – but, surely, the worn-out and the broken down virtuous married people are not the persons who should be visited with all the bitterness of an inhuman law, devised by 'expedient' politicians desirous only of serving their long train of lazy partisans.

The Brewhouse is on the back part of the building. The hop and malt are purchased and a brewer kept. He brews about once a month or five weeks. The article produced is very good – full-bodied and clean-tasted. It is not, however, every inmate that gets beer – persons at certain ages, and under certain circumstances, are regaled with John Barleycorn.

The Bakehouse is close to the last mentioned place. They bake four or five times a week, and from a sack, to a sack and an eighth per week of fine flour – the bread is good.

There are also a joiners' shop, a tailors' shop and a shoemaker's shop, in this locality, in which these businesses are carried on, and where some of the pauper youths are apprenticed. In this part, also, there are several small rooms, where old men and women live, each occupying one room, and one of them was the well-known Gage, alias Vulcan – the old man is 83 years of age and looks very happy. He said 'I am very comfortable, thank God, I have been here six years.'

At the head of the Boy's playing-ground – a very large open area – is the Boy's School, belonging to the Establishment, of course. It is composed of 34 scholars, varying from 14 years of age, downwards. Reading, writing, arithmetic, the maps, geography – not confined to the back alleys and bye lanes, as a certain worthy Town Councillor would have it – the whole superstructure, based upon the Scriptures. Some of the scholars, Mr Fryer, the schoolmaster, informs us, are very intelligent, while the intellect of the School, he thinks, very favourable indeed. One of the boys – Dryer – educated here, is now in the Training School, in the Cathedral Yard, and a girl, named Smith, from the Females' School, is third mistress in the Corporation School, at Bristol.

Connected with the House also are a stable, and a piggery – in the latter pigs are fed for the use of the inmates.

We now visit the *cuisine*, down stairs. The cook tells us that the two large furnaces before us will hold 150 gallons each, and that he had just boiled fifty-six gallons of pea-soup for the house today.

The Store-room, up stairs, has something of the appearance of a linen-draper's shop. Here all the materials necessary for dresses for the House, are kept, and measured out by Mrs Mason, who appears to have plenty of work and activity and ability to go through with it.

The Committee-room is a very nice place, without any extravagance; but comfortable: it looks like a place made for a 'Committee-of-Nine' our intelligent friend said, and we don't dispute it. There are several pictures hung around the walls – some of them unknown, but most of them probably benefactors. One of them, however, with Roman-like severity, was recognised as a portrait of the genius who 'brought the wind from the main organ in the Cathedral to the side pipes'. Over the fireplace is a view of the House and Grounds executed by a pauper, who evidently had a taste for the fine art, but did not understand 'perspective'.

The Brick-yard, at the back of the Boy's School-room, is quite a valuable adjunct to the establishment. It employs all of the inmates who are capable of doing any work, besides it enables the authorities to give needy labourers employment when they cannot obtain any elsewhere – they have now 17 of these persons employed, and each is paid at the rate of 5s a week, besides an allowance of a shilling a head for every child, under nine years of age, but this is limited to three children – 8s a week being the *maximum*, whatever the number of family may be. The bricks are in great demand both in Exeter and elsewhere, and the intelligent master, Mr Mason, informs us that first-class brick – a 'front brick' is 33s 4d per thousand, and the second quality at 28s 4d per thousand.

We have thus given the reader a pretty

general idea of the Work-house of this city, the nature, characters, ages, of its occupants; its customs, diet, appendages; its Schools, its industrial apartments, as well as its 'gymnasium' &c, though we have not, from want of space, been able to give any elaborate notice of it, the intelligent reader will have found sufficient facts to repay him for any time bestowed in glancing at them.

In conclusion, we have only to add, that there was a tone of cheerfulness pervading the whole house, seldom found in such establishments, while the general management, so far as we could see, might invite and defy criticism; but, of course, 'the White Slave' speaks only of what he has seen for himself, on this special occasion; it is possible that instances of bad economy and harsh treatment may co-exist with even a smiling exterior – but we neither saw it, nor have any reason to apprehend that such is the case.